How I Got Where I Am

by

Peter Perrin

The contents of this work, including, but not limited to, the accuracy of events, people, and places depicted; opinions expressed; permission to use previously published materials included; and any advice given or actions advocated are solely the responsibility of the author, who assumes all liability for said work and indemnifies the publisher against any claims stemming from publication of the work.

All Rights Reserved
Copyright © 2020 by Peter Perrin

No part of this book may be reproduced or transmitted, downloaded, distributed, reverse engineered, or stored in or introduced into any information storage and retrieval system, in any form or by any means, including photocopying and recording, whether electronic or mechanical, now known or hereinafter invented without permission in writing from the publisher.

Dorrance Publishing Co
585 Alpha Drive
Pittsburgh, PA 15238
Visit our website at *www.dorrancebookstore.com*

ISBN: 978-1-6480-4019-1
eISBN: 978-1-6480-4037-6

MY FATHER AND HIS TOWN

"When your father died, a lot of the history of this old town died with him." So were the words of a would-be comforter at my father's funeral. He was absolutely right. Unlike me, my father was a life-long resident of his "old town." He came into the world there in 1923. He felt secure and satisfied within its confines. The only time he left for any length of time was for four years during World War II. He enjoyed traveling and visited many places throughout his life, but he always looked forward to coming back home.

The "old town" is situated at an elevation of 1,499 feet above sea level. In its heyday, the peak population only hovered around 5,000 residents. Growth was stunted by the fact that it was difficult to get to, especially in the early years. Most people, and therefore businesses, preferred the valley plain to the northeast that had the Susquehanna River coursing through it. Ascending the steep winding roads from all directions to get to the "old town" was challenging, especially in the winter. One can only imagine trying to climb those steep inclines with a horse and wagon. Leaving the "old town" though is easy, it's all downhill. If you're brave or crazy enough to build up a good amount of speed coming out of town and could hug the tight corners, you could put your vehicle in neutral and coast the seven miles to where the valley plain begins. The coasting king was a friend named Dan, he became known as dare devil Dan. He and his brother Doug were the most insane drivers I have ever met. Thankfully, I had only experienced Dan's driving from a spectator's point of view, never as a passenger. At one rather raucous Sunday afternoon keg party, Dan took off in his father's Cadillac with one of the guys who thought he was pretty hot stuff behind the wheel of a car. Dan maneuvered the car from the field where the party was going on to the gravel road, fishtailing with dirt, dust, and stones flying all over the place. It was a one lane road but he drove like it was a four-lane highway easily exceeding 70 mph. When they returned about 20 minutes later, hot stuff was as white as the clouds in the sky above. At that moment, I vowed that I would never ride in a car with Dan at the wheel and never did. Dan was a good guy though. All of us liked beer, but Dan liked it a little too much. I stopped at an AA meeting facility many years after we had graduated from high school. I was there just as an observer and it was quite the experience. When I walked into the room where the meeting was going on, the air was blue from cigarette smoke. Coffee had replaced alcohol as the drink of choice and those in attendance consumed it as heartedly as they had consumed the drink they were now trying to overcome. At the meeting, I spotted Dan. He was a good 25 pounds heavier than the last time I had seen him and he had not aged well. Dan was there for support, which was commendable. He had bottomed out and was trying to salvage his life. We talked for a good while, not reveling in the past but about the future. Dan seemed serious about trying to get things straighten out. He had a wife, son, and a determination to be a good family man. I did not see Dan again after that day but am hopeful he succeeded in beating his demons.

The comforter was right in calling it this "old town." It had been founded in 1798. Many of the houses in town are nearing or exceed the century mark. My ancestors were some of its first settlers. Just prior to his death my father was its oldest resident. Things had changed dramatically during his lifetime. My father was more keenly aware of the changes than most. Now there are only a handful of families who had lived in the "old town" over 20 years. The town's makeup had been generational for so long: father, son, grandchildren, great-grandchildren, etc. The changes, like so many changes accelerated in the 1960s. The Vietnam War took away a good share of its young men, some enrolled in college hoping for an exemption from the war, many were drafted into the military, and a few sought refuge in Canada. Also contributing to the exodus was the wanderlust of youth and boredom. Those factors pretty much decimated the "old town's" young people. Living where there was little night life, job opportunities, and diversity had limited appeal to me. Fifty years later, of my generation, very few still call the "old town" home. Most would refer to it as the place they are from, not the place where they reside. My brother, who is two years younger than me, did stay around. He endured a failed marriage, raised a step-son, and eked out a living as a barber. He is quite thrifty, so despite the divorce, he was able to buy, pay for, and maintain a modesty house on the edge of town. In recent conversations with him, it seems he has finally tired of the "old town." His exodus will be to Florida when the time is right.

Reflecting back though, it was not that bad of a place to grow up. While we were somewhat isolated and restless, we were protected and free to do pretty much as we pleased. You see, the "old town" did not have a police force. There was a resident who fulfilled his dream to be a police officer when the town elders conferred the title of constable upon him. That title got him some gas money and the chance to put a siren and lights on his car. He had a regular job during the day, but his love was what he did after work. Some evenings but not every evening, he would patrol the "old town" after he got home and had dinner, usually started his rounds at 6:30 pm, by 10:00 pm, he was ready to retire for the evening in preparation for the next day's real work. His authority was extremely limited, really just a figurehead. As a result of no real police presence, we lived in a town where people were governed more by conscience rather than the long arm of the law. My friends and my conscience were not that fine-tuned in our youth.

In fact, we did things that in a town with police officers probably would have landed us in reform school or worse. One rather stupid stunt we enjoyed was making personal use of one of the "old town's" fire trucks. The fire hall, a converted old church, was one of the buildings surrounding the village green. The machinery was top notch for a small-town volunteer fire department. That was because one of the firemen worked at American LaFrance. Every once in a while, accessories for fire trucks left the plant in his lunchbox. As a result, the trucks were outfitted like ones you would see in a big city. He was quite a character. He ended up being shot by the husband of a woman he was running around with and thus ended the free accessories. Anyway, the two main fire engines were kept inside the station, but there was not enough space for the water tanker. It stayed outside year around to contend with the elements. Possibly for expedience, the keys were left in the ignition of the unlocked tanker for a quick getaway when there was a fire. Late some summer nights, the water truck would go missing from the station for an hour or two. We would enjoy a ride through the countryside. The old tanker would creep up the steep hills and race down them. Sometimes we would pull into a friend's yard with the lights flashing, waking them up from a dead sleep wondering if their house was on fire. Fortunately for us, there was never a real fire when we were borrowing the truck.

The firemen in town were all volunteers. Most of the volunteers worked a good distance from town, so if there was a fire during the day, some of the older high school students were called upon to help fight the blaze. The fire chief was a retired mechanic, so he was always present to take charge. He was overweight and afflicted with emphysema. He would huff and puff and run out of air when barking orders. He always drove the newest firetruck, whether it was the volunteers or the students who would be fighting the fire. The way he drove, he was often more of a danger than the fire. After several close calls and one accident on the way to a fire, he became not only a retired mechanic but now a retired fire chief. If a fire was any distance from town, the building was a goner. All that the firemen and others who gathered could do was watch, console the owners, and try to contain the blaze.

When I was 16-years-old, along with my best friends, Nick and Mike, we followed a fire truck to an accident. It was the first time I had ever seen someone dead. Two men had been drinking heavily and their car hit a concrete bridge. It was a direct hit on one of the bridge's pillars on the driver's side of the car. When we got there, they were prying the dead man out of the car. The passenger was lying alongside the road in shock. I remember my uncle kneeling beside him lighting a cigarette and letting him smoke as they waited for the ambulance to arrive. What we saw that night slowed down our driving, if only for a little while.

When we were not driving the water tanker, another available means of transportation was a commuter's car that would be left in front of the church on the opposite side of the village green from the fire house. Several men from the area worked at a factory about an hour's drive from the "old town" and would car pool. They worked the afternoon-evening shift, from 3:30 pm to around midnight, and they would not return to the "old town" before 1:00 am. The trusting owner of a 1964 Ford Falcon would put his keys under the front seat of his unlocked car. Week nights after the constable retired, the car was at our disposal for a couple of hours. Nick was usually the one who drove as he was good shifting a manual transmission. All we had to do was make sure the car was back by 12:30 am, so the engine could cool down and the owner would be none the wiser. As the owner was a non-smoker, we were smart enough not to smoke in his car. This provision continued to be available right through my senior year in high school. After school Mike went into the navy and Nick and I started working different jobs, he at a feed mill and me at a factory that made televisions. It was not long before Nick and I could make our first major purchase and each of us bought a car. Needless to say, we kept them under lock and key when not in use.

On the matter of not smoking in the commuter's car, the opposite was true when we had Nick's grandmother's car, an old Desoto. One night Nick, Mike, Chilson Vanderpool, and myself all lit up cigars in her car with the windows up and waited to see who would be the first one to bail out. I forget who first bailed, but when the doors finally did fly open, it looked like the car was on fire as thick cigar smoke bellowed from it. Our clothes, hair, and bodies reeked of the smell of tobacco for the rest of the evening, the car reeked for several days thereafter. The first thing Chilson did after he got out of the car was light up a cigarette.

One night the constable gave us a close call. It happened in the late fall of my junior year. The asphalt road ended about 100 yards after you passed the cemetery leaving the "old town" going north. Mike, Nick and I were about ¾ of a mile up from the cemetery on the graveled part of the road parked in the driveway of an abandoned trailer. The location was halfway up the steep hill from the cemetery at a turn in the road. We had limited vision in both directions. The purpose of our parking out in the middle of nowhere was to enjoy some liquid refreshment that none of us were legally old enough to indulge in at the time. Acquiring alcohol though was not difficult. We would use the commuter car, drive to one of the valley towns, and make our purchase. We would buy a fairly good quantity and stash a reserve in locations around the "old town" for those occasions when we didn't have transportation. The "old town" was dry with the exception of the VFW hall. The drinking age at the time was 18 years of age. I had been shaving since I was 13-years-old. By 16, if I skipped shaving for several days, heavy whiskers gave me the appearance of someone much older. I was usually the one who was recruited to go into a store to make the purchase. If you went to the right places, there was little danger of being asked to show your identification and we knew the right places. The first few purchases, my heart raced as I went to the cooler, picked up several six-packs of beer, and headed for the counter. It was not long before I was on a first name basis with the proprietor. It was obvious he was more concerned about profit than the age of the purchaser. That night we were in Nick's parent's car, a Pontiac GTO. This was a rare treat. It was cold, so we were in the car listening to the radio drinking and smoking cigarettes rather than sitting on the hood of the car as we would do in warmer weather. Suddenly, lights shot up the road as the constable's car came around the corner. He drove past the driveway where we were parked, saw us, slammed on his brakes, and put his car in reverse. Before the constable could back up and block our escape, Nick started the car and we were on the gravel in an instant. As he put the gas pedal to the floor, stones and gravel were flying all over the place. These pelted the back end of the constable's car busting out his taillights. Before he could get turned around, we were well on our way in the opposite direction. We reveled in triumph as we sped off into the night, of course with the headlights off so the constable could not get a good look at the car's license plate. The downside of our triumph was that we had to find another spot to enjoy our libations when the constable was on duty. He made cruising past our old haunt part of his regular patrol from that night on. These were some on the milder stunts life in a town with no real police presence made possible and unpunishable.

Calling the "old town" unassuming would be an accurate description. I lived in the Ohio Valley for several years and was amazed, as well as amused how local folk heroes were lauded. A lot of prominent athletes heralded from that area. Usually at all points of entry into their "old towns" were signs proclaiming "the home of (supply the name of the local hero)." One town made one of its dwellings famous as the place where Clark Gable was born. He never lived there, I guess his mother was just passing through when Clark was ready to come into the world and the rest is history.

There was none of that in my father's "old town." The streets had rather bland names, Main, Water, Church, and School, nothing fancy or imaginative. It was not that the "old town" lacked notable residents. There were ones who gained prominence in the fields of science, medicine, and sports, but their accomplishments were not singled out any more than that of the farmer or laborer who stayed in the area, worked hard, and raised a respectable family. The only thing that bears a person's name in the "old town" is the Gladys P. Childress elementary school. Miss Childress, as she was addressed by young and old alike, served as first grade teacher and principal of the elementary school. She remained single her entire life and devoted over 50 years to educating the "old town's" young people. She was charitable with her time and money in promoting projects that enhanced the town and benefited its residents. This probably was the reason tradition was broken and she was given special recognition and honor. One of my earliest memories of attending the Gladys P. Childress elementary school happened in first grade. I was six-years-old. We students were outside on the playground for recess. I was with my friend Sydney on the swing set that day, it was in the fall shortly after the school year had started. Her mother and my mother were not from the "old town," they grew up together in one of the nearby valley towns. They were close and so visited often. Sydney and I crawled together, learned to walk together, and enjoyed playing together. I viewed her as a good friend. All that changed on the swing that day. We were swinging having a wonderful time, seeing how high we could soar. Then came the call, "Recess is over. Time to go inside." As we got off the swing, Sydney kissed me on the cheek and ran into the school. I was stunned and furious! I could not get to the boys' room fast enough to wash my face. After that day, Sydney was no longer my bud and we never really regained the closeness we experienced before the kiss. She excelled in school; in our junior year, she lived in Sweden for a year as an exchange student. I never even inquired about her experiences or her impression of the place when she returned. My loss in looking back. I have no idea what Sydney is doing today but am quite certain whatever it is, she is very successful.

My father was like the town he grew up in, very unassuming. I totally misunderstood him when growing up. Neil Young sang a song entitled, "Old Man." He encouraged his old man to take a look at his life. As I have grown older, I realize the aged are capable of doing that. It's the young who have the problem of looking at their elders' life. A serious lack of wisdom and experience hindered me from really understanding things properly. In reflecting back on the 1960's, me and my peers felt so enlightened and loving, when in reality, we were many times just the opposite. We felt endowed with such great intellect so much so that we could solve the world's problems. About all we did was contribute to them, along with finding fault with those who did try to make a better planet. I look back now and think, you fool.

My father's humility was genuine. He was a responsible person who took good care of his family materially and was generally a kind, pleasant soul to be around. He had a well-deserved reputation of being a slow driver. At times it was frustrating riding in the car with him, everyone would pass you by. I never remember my father passing anyone when he drove.

When my mother would ride with me, although I would be driving the speed limit, she would say, "Aren't we going a little too fast?" My father was the picture of patience. There was an old farmer near town who was just the opposite. His name was Ed Sprouse. He hated to be passed on the highway. Once a driver passed him about a ¼ of a mile before an intersection with a stop sign. Ed repassed the driver before they got to the stop sign. Ed was not one to be toyed with on the highway or one you preferred to ride with either. He did though make a respectable hard cider. Each year he would do up four large wooden barrels of the brew to carry him through the year. He added a hefty amount of raisins to enhance the alcoholic content. Ed was very generous with and proud of his cider.

When it was ready in the late fall, Mike, Nick and I would pay him a visit to sample his cider. He was more than willing to allow us to do so. He and his wife never had children, but they took a real liking to my younger sister and treated her royally. Having no heirs, Ed and his wife left their farm to the town and it was turned into a park. A fine deed by a decent man and woman.

GRANDFATHER AND GRANDMOTHER

My father, as was true of others who live during the 1920s and 30s, was not one to waste money. Later in life though, he did enjoy weekly trips to a casino about an hour from his home. He was well disciplined with his gambling, never losing more than $50 a visit, he set a limit and knew when to quit. My mother liked to pull the handles as well.

My father's work ethic and conservatism reflected the environment he was raised in. His father, my grandfather, whom I never met as he died prior to my being born, took the risk of giving up a job that paid $63 a month to open a general store in the "old town." That was not viewed as a prudent move by most at that time, but his gamble paid off. His adventurous spirit ended up providing a good living for him, my grandmother, father, and his older brother, Luther . Luther was 13 years older than my father. My grandfather was able to send him to medical school, as he was an excellent student. Luther excelled and became a fairly redounded physician. Also testifying to my grandfather's success was the fact my grandmother lived on for 25 years after his death and never had to go to work secularly.

Going through some family records, I came across a copy of my grandfather's will. His wishes showed him to be a very fair man. His will stipulated that $10,000, a large sum of money at that time, be given to my father. This equaled the amount he spent sending Luther to college and medical school. My grandmother was also a very kind, generous person. Late in her life, she sold my father the house he was born, grew up, and died in for one dollar. She, too, died in that house. After the purchase, my father added on to the house and grandmother lived with us in the old part and we in the new. I have many fond memories of living under the same roof with her. We would watch baseball games together on a black and white television set in her bedroom. She knew the game well and was an avid hater of the New York Yankees, something I inherited from her. The only time I ever heard her curse was watching a baseball game. Before she died, she got a color television and marveled when she saw the bright blue water beyond Candlestick Park during the 1962 World Series between the San Francisco Giants and the hated ones. Of course, she was highly upset with the Giants for losing game seven that year. As the oldest grandson, I think I had a special place in her heart. To me it seemed she spent a lot more time with me than her other grandchildren. A fond remembrance I have is of a poem she helped me compose, truth is she did most of the composing. In fifth grade, the class was assigned to write a report about a famous poet and his or her works. I let the teacher know there was not a poet I felt inclined to report on. He gave me an alternative; if you do not write a report, write a poem. I accepted the challenge. Grandmother and I worked on a poem about fall. All I remember about the poem was the line, "the frost is on the pumpkins, the leaves are falling fast." James Taylor's song, "Walking Man," has the lyrics "the frost is on the pumpkins" in it. I think he must have gotten it from grandmother and me. Anyway, the poem was a success, it was published in the school paper and I got high marks for it thanks to my grandmother.

I can clearly recall the night she died. It was a Saturday night, my wife and I were out with my cousin and his girlfriend. A couple of hours into our evening, my cousin's father contacted him and told him we needed to get home right away, no explanation as to why, just get home. We were visiting my parents and grandmother that weekend. Our infant son was at the house, my younger sister was enjoying the opportunity to babysit him. Racing through my mind were all kinds of bad thoughts, thinking that something had happened to him. When we pulled up, the street was busy and there was an ambulance parked right in front of the house. I sprinted to the house and was relieved to find my son okay but troubled that my grandmother had died. It really should not have come as a big surprise as she had declining health for years. Several strokes had left her able to climb the stairs to her second floor bedroom only once a day. She no longer had the energy to clean, wash, cook, or perform any of the domestic duties she had excelled at earlier in life. She had lost the will to live; on more than one occasion, I heard her say she was ready and wanted to die. In looking back and considering her quality of life, or rather her lack of a quality life, her dying was overdue. In a sense, she had really stopped living years before. At that time though, I was thinking more of myself than of her and that is why the experience proved so distressing. A small consolation was she died at home, never having to live in a convalescent home, as nursing home were referred to then. Hers was the second funeral I remember attending. The first was my best friend, Nick's father, who died when we were both 15 years old.

A day of visitation by friends, acquaintances, and family preceded my grandmother's funeral, which was conducted three days after she died. By this time, I was more objective in my thinking. The service took place at the funeral home in the "old town," a block off the village green. Family representatives from the majority of the townspeople attended. The men wore suits and ties, the woman dresses, their Sunday best. Many of the men who grew up with my father were totally out of their element in a suit but donned one out of respect. My grandfather had extended credit to many of the "old town's" residents during hard times. One of my father's closest friends was orphaned when a teenager. My grandfather was one of the few that extended him a helping hand. He provided him with work and credit, despite his being of rough character and reputation. He turned out to be a solid citizen and good family man. It's possibly he could have played professional baseball had it not been for World War II. His bond with my father was genuine, they were like brothers. He was there for my father and to pay his respects to the woman who had become like a mother to him. This fine man took in foster children during the time his two boys were growing up. It showed the acts of kindness extended to him when he was young were not wasted or unappreciated.

All the people present were very polite and expressed sincere sentiments as they passed through the receiving line. Most said something kind and personal about my grandmother. Their expressions were out of respect for someone who had been a pillar and model citizen in the "old town." Because of her age and poor health, no one was overcome with extreme sadness. In fact most were having a good time reminiscing. My uncle Luther, who I would see twice a year, once when we took grandmother to his home for three months in the winter, and the second time when we would pick her up in the spring, seemed to be having a particularly good time. Here was an opportunity for him to visit with ones he knew growing up but had not seen for years. It must have appeared strange to his two adult daughters. As a doctor, he had provided them with a lot of material comforts, culture, and education. The number of times they had visited the "old town" could have been counted on one hand. When they did visit, their stay was usually no more than half a dozen hours. Here was their father, a sophisticated physician very much at ease and enjoying the company of people, the type of who they had never seen their father associate with in their town. The only one I observed who was solemn and subdued was my father. He was deeply affected by the loss. I came to understand that my grandmother was like an anchor for him. I believe he talked more with her than with my mother. Because he came along later in her life, there was a kind of Sarah and Isaac connection. To say his world was rocked would be an understatement. Luther cast a long shadow and I could tell he felt somewhat inferior when around him. He clumsily would try to say something profound to impress Luther. Mother's know this about their sons and I think she loved him the more. This woman who bolstered his spirit, instilled confidence and self-worth in him would no longer be there to turn to when his soul became troubled. She was going to be and was sadly missed by my father.

THE FUNERAL

It was a gorgeous day in May, leaves not yet on all the trees, but the early spring flowers were in bloom, the winds were tame, and the sun warm. Like the town and my father, the cemetery was unassuming. It bore the plain, simple sign at its entrance stating it was the Union Cemetery. It was quite large, as there were more residents in the dust than in the town. It is situated on a knoll to the north of the village green. The tombstones are set in no particular pattern, nor are the rows straight. It is a caretaker's nightmare to mow. Most of the oldest tombstones are so badly weathered that the lettering is not readable. The most antiquated legible marker is for a Sarah Al.... The date of her passing was September 11th, 1808. The trees randomly scattered throughout the grounds are mainly maples. My family's plot is at one of the highest points in the cemetery. Beautiful views delight the eyes in three of four directions. North, you look into a dense woods, especially specular in the fall of the year. Look west and you see a picturesque valley with several small farms in the distance. South, you observe the upper part of the "old town." The centerpiece is the village green flanked on the east by one of the town's oldest churches and at one time a century old bank. The building was tore down when the "old town" bank was merged with a larger, supposedly more progressive one that liked to have all its buildings look the same. Some of the older residents lamented the destruction but their memory is short. It was not an easy place for all to enter. The steps you had to ascend to get into the old bank were steep and many. This proved a real challenge for the lame, handicap, and elderly, which describes a lot of the "old town's" residents. In the old days, anyone in those categories was allowed to go behind the bank, go in through the back door at ground level, precede through the bank president's office, and walk up to one of the teller stations. The bank president, Dent Bagley, was the same way when he would go to my father's general store to get his mail. The post office was located at the store and took up about a quarter of the store's floor space. There was a partition and door that isolated the post office from the rest of the store. Of course, anyone could see what was going on inside the post office as there was a series of huge glass windows that ran the full length of the front of the store. The porch also ran the entire length of the store's front. The windows were at a height of about three feet above the porch floor. Usually there were bags of animal feed in front of the windows. Men would sit on these and converse. The postmaster, Ernie, my father's partner in the store, was like a fish in a bowl. One and all could watch his every move. The bank president paid no attention to protocol, you could tell that by the way he ran the bank. He was an outstanding judge of character though. After a brief conversation and promise of repayment, a loan was usually given. Loans were granted in good faith, no long forms to fill out or background checks, dealing with him was quick and easy, in and out in 30 minutes, leaving with check in hand.

When Dent came to the store, rather than opening the door of his box on the outside, he would walk into the mail room, get his mail, the banks', and any neighbors who asked him to get theirs. Dent and Ernie were good friends and would engage each other in conversation, sometimes long, other times brief. Dent finished his visit by having a Coke and then it was time to get back to the bank. This was his routine each weekday. It would have been easy for him to send one of the tellers for the mail, but he enjoyed the excursion. His routine though was not well received when the postal inspector would make his annual visit to go over government records and protocol with Ernie. There was a look of shock on the inspector's face when Dent pranced into the mail room during the inspection. Ernie got a rather strong reprimand afterward for running such a lax operation. The next day, when the Dent came, the inspector was still there going over the records, this time Ernie locked the door and Dent had to go to the counter window like everyone else to get his mail. Of course, after the postal inspector completed his work and left, it was back to business as usual until the next annual inspection.

Getting back to the view, the view to the east was an eyesore. Drilling for natural gas had become very profitable in the area. As a result, the landscape in many areas changed drastically. This was true of the scenery in that direction, it was now marred by the sight of gas pads, wells, and water trucks. All things considered though, three out of four pleasing vantage points is not too bad.

    I was in charge of picking up my mother and getting her to the cemetery that day. This proved to be quite an ordeal, as she was no longer good at remembering details, times, places, etc. With my wife's help, we managed to arrive in time for the service with several minutes to spare. The mood at the cemetery was more festive than mournful. Much like my grandmother's funeral. One of the big differences though was the casualness of the occasion compared to the formal feel at grandmother's funeral. Here the dress of the day was khakis, golf shirts, and ball caps for the men. Most of the ladies wore slacks and light jackets. There were only five males who wore dress suits. Myself, a nephew whose suit was more of a fashion statement, a Mianite boy who helped my father with his yardwork, a cousin who was running for county judge and would do a little campaigning later at the reception, and lastly the minister who was scheduled to speak. My father had died in January and it was his desire to have a graveside service rather than a church ceremony. January is not too conducive for a grave side funeral at this latitude. The time between his death in January and his burial in May had taken the edge off any immense sorrow anyone had. My brother who handled all the arrangements decided the first Saturday in May would work well and he was right. Present for the occasion were about 70 of the townsfolks and the rest were family, ones who were close and others not so close, but they were there to pay their respects as my father had done for so many of their loved ones. In all about 100 attended. My father had a large number of friends and acquaintances throughout his life, but by the time he died, most of his contemporaries had preceded him to the grave. My brother called the service to order, announcing the events to follow. He was the picture of casualness wearing an open collar white shirt, new blue jeans, and walking around sipping liquid from a Pepsi can, soda I presumed. First up were representatives from the Masonic Temple. My father was a member but not an active one. I never remembered him talking about the organization, but he did wear their ring on special occasions. The fact that the main spokesman for the group kept calling him "brother" rather than addressing him by name was a pretty good indication of his lack of participation in the organization. Next were six older veterans from the American Legion. They presented my mother with a flag and expressed the gratitude of the nation for my father's participation in World War II. It, too, was rather impersonal as my father was again referred to as "brother." One member about 50 feet away from the main party softly played taps in the shadow of a large maple tree. Following this was a 21 gun salute. Later my brother gathered up some of the shells and buried them along with our father's ashes. Last to speak was his minister. To his credit, he brought a personal touch to the occasion. He spoke about how when he first moved to the "old town," it was my father who served as historian and quasi-advisor about matters pertaining to the town and the church where he would be ministering. After that my brother brought things to a close, inviting all in attendance to go to the town hall to enjoy fellowship and a barbeque dinner. It was a nice opportunity to do what my uncle did at my grandmother's funeral, see old acquaintances, and do some reminiscing. The ones I felt compelled to speak to were the few peers of my father that were present. It had been difficult for some of them to attend with failing health, physical limitations, and little energy. They seemed to be enjoying themselves but I have to believe they must have given thought to how in the not too distant future a gathering like this would be held for their families. The Mianite boy and his sister did not come to the dinner. I was touched by the fact that he and she were at the funeral. My parents had always treated him kindly and paid him handsomely when he came to the house to help my father with his yardwork and other chores. They also made sure that before he left, he was well fed. My brother showed his appreciation by giving him some of my parent's household goods at a ridiculously low price. He could have included them with their other possessions that were auctioned off two years later on Labor Day weekend. It was a nice gesture by my brother. Absent from the funeral was my father's best living friend, Charles. They had been close since childhood and both were in their 90s when my father died. It was not that Charles was unable to get around, but he had become somewhat of a recluse in his old age. My father had taken over his father's general store after his death cutting short a military career. In the back of the store was the soda machine, the location served as the social center for farmers in the area. Along with the soda machine in the cramped corner were three benches, and the place of honor, a coveted rocking chair. Charles would often hold court there for about an hour each day. He would usually arrive early to lay claim to the rocking chair and consume two or three Cokes during his stay. Later in life, he switched to drinking Pepsi. My father always joined in the robust conversations when he was not occupied with waiting on customers. He reveled in such opportunities, here were gathered men who had known each other from childhood, and in their own peculiar way, loved one another, though they would never admit to or show it. Ironically, Charles had only been in my father's house once. He drove a worn-out antiquated Chevy pickup around the "old town." If he would see my father working in the yard or sitting on the front porch, he would stop and they would enjoy each other's company for an hour or more. This took place about twice a week on average during the spring, summer, and fall. The severe winter months would interrupt their visits, but come spring, Charles would be back. I happened to be at the house the one time Charles came inside. My father was losing his battle against heart disease and Charles came to the door to see how he was doing. He was heartedly invited in by my mother. She, too, enjoyed conversing with Charles. My father's bed had been moved downstairs into the living room. He was no longer able to talk and seemed little aware of what was happening around him. Charles spoke, mostly with my mother, for about half an hour or so.

When he left, he went over to my father's bed and said, "Eagle, I will see you later, take care." I think he knew that was the last time he would see my father alive. I was intrigued by his calling my father "Eagle." It was the first and only time I heard him called that. I am disappointed I did not follow Charles out and ask him about the "Eagle" expression. One of my uncles at the funeral said he was surprised not to see Charles present. I was not, that is the way Charles is. I wholeheartedly believe he showed up after everyone left the cemetery and had his final talk with "Eagle."

The one who was like my father at his mother's funeral was my sister's oldest son Porter. She had two sons who were complete opposites. My father had become, in a sense, Porter's father as well as his grandfather as my sister divorced when he was young and Porter's father was more interested in the ladies than in him. He had a special place in my father's heart and Porter had a deep sense of loyalty toward him even as a youth. His brother, Donald, was more like my uncle, scholarly and socially skilled. Porter mirrored my father, one who worked with his hands and enjoyed doing so. He had achieved his lifelong desire to be a farmer and was at peace tilling the soil. My father was never one to openly show his affection. When Porter was a baby though, he would take him in his arms and coddle him. I never remember experiencing that or seeing my siblings experience that. There was a strong bond between the two. My father would take Porter with him to deliver cow feed to farmers in the outlying areas around the "old town." That is where the seeds were planted with Porter's love for farming. My father did everything he could to make up for Porter not having a father figure at home to learn from. He might have also been making up for the time he did not spend with my brother and me when we were young. As I stated earlier, he was a good provider. To accomplish that, he worked at his store and also had a second, more profitable job that he worked from early afternoon to midnight. It was factory work. He originally took the job when I was around ten-years-old. He planned on working there for 5 years but stayed for 25. As a result, we saw little of him when growing up. He was not going to let the opportunity to spend time with Porter escape him. Their closeness was clearly shown when my father had a heart attack earlier in life. Porter was nine-years-old when it happened and he went to visit my father in the hospital and sobbed on his shoulder uncontrollably as my father lay in bed. Porter visited his grandfather two days before he died, now he was married and had a son of his own. I was not there when he arrived. When I did get there, here was Porter again sobbing at his grandfather's bedside, holding his hand, this time accompanied by his wife, who was also in tears. Her sorrow came from seeing her grief-stricken husband rather than the dire condition of his grandfather. My father was unable to speak, but his eyes were fixated on Porter. Before Porter left, my father's lips moved, forming the silent words "I love you." None of us present, my sister, my mother, or me had ever heard him utter those words before. It was very touching, especially for Porter.

I watched him at the funeral. The man who bolstered his spirit, instilled confidence and self-worth in him would no longer be there for him to turn to when his soul became troubled. He was going to be sadly missed by all but especially by Porter. After the ceremony, Porter walked off by himself into a secluded area of the cemetery looking very melancholy. His wife eventually went over to console him and led him back to the gathering. His eyes were red. I felt for him.

THE CONTRAST

My mother died approximately three years after my father. Her last three years were not pleasant. She enjoyed being a house keeper, cooking, washing, all the things wives and mothers did so well in the 1950s and 60s. Her battle with dementia curtailed those activities. Her final days were spent in a personal care facility in the valley town she grew up in. She was joined there by her fleshy brother, Max, who was battling the same dreaded disease. My brother worked up the block from where our mother then lived. He would stop to check on her before he went to work in the morning and after he closed the doors to his barber shop at night. He did this five days a week. He made sure to schedule her medical appointments on his days off so he could accompany her and communicate with her doctors. I was living out of the area at this time. My visits were bi-monthly and she remembered me right up to until the last few visits I made. My brother was excellent at keeping my sister and me abreast of how our mother was doing. He would also let me know how her finances were holding up and would ask for my input on decisions of that nature. I do not believe he shared that information with my sister as they had a tendency to quarrel over such matters. My brother confided in me that he had promised our father when he was dying, that he would take good care of our mother and he did. Before the family house was sold after my mother went to live at the personal care facility, he worked tirelessly, keeping the place looking nice and maintaining it. As winter was approaching the second year the house was empty, he decided to auction off the house and its belongings. That was a good decision on his part and I am glad as it removed the burden of trying to care for two places from him. Growing up I was never close with my brother, but my respect for him soared with the responsibility he took on caring for our parents in their last years. I regularly would let him know how much I appreciated all he was doing. After our mother died, my brother did something I never thought he would do. He moved away from the "old town" and took up residence in Florida. He had previously talked of doing that, but I never took him seriously. For a man who could account for every dollar he made and spent, he showed a benevolent spirit when he left the "old town." He gave his adopted step-son his home and the Mianite boy who helped my father around the house and attended his and my mother's funerals, some of their material possessions.

The contrast between the funerals of my father and mother were as different as night and day. Where my father's was a rather festive occasion with a good size attendance and the previously described ceremonies, my mother's was somber, sad, and only attended by a few close family members. My father had been in fairly good health up until the last six months of his life.

Memories of him were mostly positive, life was good for him. He was able to do his yardwork, which he loved, he and mother continued to make their weekly trips to the casino, and he was still able to enjoy the association of several of the peers who he grew up with. My mother's final years were not that kind. Dementia robbed her of a quality life. As time wore on, she spent more and more time in bed. No desire to read, communicate with others, the simple pleasure of eating had loss it appeal. She would have worn the same clothes everyday had it not been for my brother making sure the staff assisted her with caring for her hygiene. My mother's younger sister by two years, Barbara, was loyal and loving to her. Even though mother would forget you had visited her five minutes after you left, Barbara went to see her religiously two times a week. She and her ill husband, Harvey, would winter in Florida, but she called often to speak with her sister and inquire from my brother how things were going. She also made sure to visit her brother, Max, when she came to see my mother. They had another brother, Phil, who was also good about stopping by to see his siblings on a regular basis. Phil was like the candy man, always bringing chocolate bars and other goodies to his brother and sister. Phil had his share of health problems over the years, but at present, his cancer was in remission and he was living a fairly active life. I'm sure he was doing everything he could to keep from becoming a resident at the personal care facility; to visit was one thing, to live there, another. Phil was quite a successful businessman. He had a strong desire to be a politician. He made it to being president of the Young Republicans club for his county but was badly defeated in the two elections he ran in for county commissioner.

That was a position I feel my father could have ascended to had he had the desire. He was well connected with ones who had a lot of political influence and his personality would have made him a popular candidate. I recall Phil gathering my brother, two of my cousins, and me to do door-to-door canvasing for him during his first campaign. Our job was mainly to pass out fliers heralding his accomplishments and virtues. It was an interesting experience but one I had no desire to repeat and so was a non-participant in his second bid for county commissioner. My mother's youngest brother, Jake, the one who asked about Charles at my father's funeral, would visit from time to time. He was 15 years younger than my mother. Their mother died when Jake was 14-years-old and his father had preceded her to the grave. Jake, Max, and Phil lived together until Max got married and Jake went off to college. Max went to work at the local Sylvania factory and worked there for close to 40 years. Phil later went to work at the same factory, he and Max made a lot of sacrifices for Jake. As best as two young men could do, they made sure Jake had life's necessities and that he did well in school. He was the only one in the family of seven who went to college. Jake is a fine example of what hard work and dedication can accomplish. He got his degree in education and became a teacher and later a school superintendent for the good part of three decades. My mother and Barbara played a big role in caring for their three younger brothers. Especially was their care appreciated when it came to cooking, sewing, and some financial help. By this world's standards, they were a very close knit and caring family.

In attendance at my mother's funeral was my brother and sister, Phil, Barbara, and Jake. Max and Harvey were too ill to attend. The graveside service took about 15 minutes, whereas my father's lasted well over an hour. There were no American Legion soldiers, no gun salute, taps, or Masons. The Mianite boy who worked for my parents read a few select scriptures from the Psalms, told the attendees that Jesus loved them, and mother was now in a good place in heaven, he said a prayer, and that was it. Whereas the mood at my father's funeral was light hearted and jovial, at my mother's, it was somber and sad. Afterward, there was no barbeque dinner, just burying my mother's ashes beside her husband. Everyone spoke cordially to each other at the cemetery for about 15 minutes after the service and then left. No tears but a real sense of sadness as to how my mother finished her life. I have not returned to the "old town" since and have little motivation to at present. I probably will before my appointment with the grave, to do a little reflecting. My brother has several plots at the Union Cemetery and offered me one. That is not my preferred way to return to the "old town."

ONE LIFE OVER ONE JUST BEGINNING

I once heard someone say they wished they could have been a grandparent before they were a parent. No doubt they would have been a better parent. I concur with that assessment. My wife and I have one granddaughter, Ruthie. She lives on the west coast and we on the east coast, so visits are few and far apart. I am envious of but happy for grandparents who see and spend time with their grandchildren on a regular basis. I would love to see Ruthie every day. We Skype when possible. She is seven-years-old, a very active seven-year-old. She loves riding horses, (something inherited from her mother), swimming, and doing all the California things. She is quite an accomplished horse rider for a seven-years-old. My wife and I watched her practice when we last visited. Before riding, she led her horse, Daisy, out of the stable to the saddling area. There was a little platform for her to stand on. Daisy was positioned next to the platform. This made it easy for Ruthie to mount her. After riding Daisy around the ring for about 30 minutes, doing paces and jumping some low railings, she rode Daisy back to the platform and dismounted. Then she cleaned her horse's shoes, hosed her down, brushed her, and led her back to the stable. I was very impressed. I'm sure after that kind of excitement Skyping with the grandparents is pretty anticlimactic. We appreciate the opportunities though and love her dearly.

Ruthie, like many children today, is experiencing something that was totally foreign to me and most of my peers. My parents had been married for 68 years when my father died, my wife and I have been married for 46. I am a firm believer in commitment and loyalty to a marriage mate. My son and Ruthie's mother divorced when Ruthie was four and a half-years-old. I can only imagine how confusing that must be for a little child. It is obvious that both parents deeply love their daughter, but somewhere along the way, they fell out of love with one another. Commendably, my son has remained in California to be an active part of his daughter's life. Financially and emotionally, it has to be hard, but it's well worth the sacrifice. Ruthie appears to be resilient and enjoys the time she spends with each parent, but it has to be strange as to why they don't spend time together as a family like they used to. My job is not to judge, just do what I can to try and be a positive influence in her young life.

I am glad my parents got a few opportunities to see Ruthie before they died. They had an old orange rotary telephone and no internet service, so Skyping was out of the question for them. She was their first great-grandchild. My son was the only great-grandchild my grandmother ever saw, albeit it was briefly. As I mentioned earlier, he was just an infant when she died. I doubt

I will ever see a great-grandchild as I am now in my seventies. No need to lament what you never had though.

Ruthie is in a Spanish immersion school, very cool. She talks about doing time lincs in Spanish, whatever they are, and receiving high marks for her efforts. I do not remember much about being seven-years-old and certainly nothing about receiving high marks, except for the poem my grandmother and I composed. I would have been in second grade at that age. What I remember about second grade is that it was not much fun. Kindergarten was the fun. We had an elderly teacher in kindergarten, Miss Meyers, who was more babysitter than teacher. My memories of kindergarten were of playing all day and running away from Miss Meyers when she try to get her hands on you and give you what she called a tin ear. It was a brutal upward twist of the ear. Because our elementary school was being renovated when I was in kindergarten, our class met in the VFW hall. We were upstairs and the bar was downstairs, but it was off limits to members during school hours. Despite the hardship, the members considered it their civic duty to sacrifice for the "old town's" children.

Another recollection I have of kindergarten is the day a dead beaver showed up in class. In the "old town" were two old fleshly brothers, the Smith brothers, who were lifelong bachelors. They lived simply in an old but adequate mobile home. Their later days were filled with hunting, fishing, and trapping. Earlier in life, they had a success sawmill, which they sold for a handsome sum. The older brother, Fred, was checking his traps one cold December morning and discovered a beaver. This was highly unusual and he felt worthy of being shown to the townsfolks. After a visit to my father's store and the bank, the beaver made its way to the VFW. The reason why Fred was welcome to show his beaver at the bank was because the Smith brothers were one of the bank's biggest depositors having saved most of their money from the sale of the sawmill. Dent was more than willing to put up with the show and tell rather than risk offending one of the bank's largest depositors.

The beaver was rolled in on a gurney with Fred standing proudly at its side. He opened the beaver's mouth to show the children its teeth. The trap wounds were gory and the creature was blood stained. Today, parents would be mortified if such a showing were to take place at their child's school. Back then no one thought anything of it. The boys were excited to see the beaver and the girls were grossed out by it.

The girls being grossed out reminds me of another incident in kindergarten. We had a classmate named Lyman. He had two older brothers and all three were extremely visually impaired. Lyman had a glass eye. He would take it out and chase the girls around the classroom. They would run screaming as we boys cheered Lyman on. Miss Meyers was never amused by Lyman's antics. He received the dreaded tin ear on numerous occasions. In high school, Lyman turned out to be a pretty good wrestler. He made it to the district finals his junior and senior years but ran up against a very skilled and stronger wrestler both times. Lyman left the "old town" to attend college, which is how he made his exodus.

Back to Ruthie. She will probably be the last one bearing the family name, although that is no big deal. Everything we know now has a beginning and an end. My hope is that my wife and

I live long enough so she can gain some memories of us to reflect on later in her life as I have reflected on my grandmother. She was the only grandparent I knew and my life would not have been as rich had I not had the opportunity to spend time with her. Now though it's time to move on to some lighter stories.

THE CLEANERS

In my late 20s, I lived in one of the valley towns for several years. It was a pleasant experience and I made some great friends. One especially good friend, Chuck and I started a janitorial business. It did well enough for us to hire another friend, Doug. Most of our work was in the evening and early morning hours. A work night would start with cleaning the office area of an ironworks foundry. The black sand from the plant filtered through the air, made its way into the office area, making it difficult to leave the clean sterile environment we said our service could deliver in our advertisements. The human resource manager was a reasonable man, he understood our dilemma and did not expect the impossible. Next stop was the First National Bank. Totally opposite situation, in and out in 45 minutes and lots of praise from the manager. He proved to be a good source as a reference for future clients. Around 10:00 pm, it was time to clean a combination bakery, restaurant, small grocery store. This was the most pleasant stop of the evening. When we arrived the night baker would just be starting his shift. His main job was making donuts. He had to have a hundred dozen or more ready for deliver by 3:00 am. He was very generous with the owner goods. Every night he made sure we enjoyed hot buttermilk donuts with a cold glass of milk before we left for the last job of the night. For a short while, the last stop was a job that we worked for only two weeks. It was a tavern on Main Street called the Wander Inn. I guess the suggestion being to wander in for a drink. In reality for most, it was wander in and stagger out. The state law was for the last drinks to be served at 1:00 am and everyone gone by 1:30 am. At the Wander Inn all that closed at 1:30 am were the shades. Business would go on until the last customer was either out of money or out of his mind drunk. The straw that broke the camel's back with that job happened the second Friday night of our brief employment there. Playing darts was a popular pastime in area taverns. There was a dart league with taverns sponsoring their own teams. They would have competing home-away contests rotating between taverns. On this particular night, we arrived about 1:30 am after enjoying the peace and tranquility of the bakery. Greeting us were the team captains wrestling on the floor to the cheers and encouragement of their teammates. In the dart room was a drunken shooter standing with his hand on the dart board and fingers spread wide apart. An equally drunk shooter was attempting to throw darts between his fingers. We got there just in time to see the shooter miss and harpoon the index finger of his drunken comrade. At that point, we informed the owner that our contract with him had expired and there would be no two weeks' notice. That experience led to an agreement that there would be no future cleaning of taverns. The funny thing is that a mere ten years earlier, I would have relished that kind of revelry.

As my mother would say, "You've got to get it out of your system." Time has proved the wisdom of moderation to me. Also I see no conceivable reason to use tobacco, even in moderation although I once enjoyed that vice. I stayed with my father and mother for a month before my father died. During that time and shortly afterward, the names of four men I was close to growing up appeared in the obituary column of the local newspaper. Just recently my brother informed me of a fifth who died of cancer. All were lifelong smokers and heavy drinkers. One of them was Nick. We were born two weeks apart, he being the older. We lived on the same street, there were six houses between us. We were inseparable growing up but had drifted in different directions after we graduated from high school. His travels eventually led him to Alaska, where he lived for 30 years. I have lived in nine different states, mostly in the Mid-West, though I currently call Massachusetts home and I love it here. Nick returned to the "old town" for the first time in 14 years to see his mother and remaining family members. He stayed three weeks, went back to Alaska, and died a month later. That was pause for some serious reflection. Life's brevity makes me want to use it wisely. I guess I got "it out of my system."

Another cleaning experience I would like to relate shows how dangerous an occupation it can be. Chuck and I agreed to help out a fellow competitor with stripping and waxing the floor of a large department store he had contracted. It was an exhausting job that took four nights to finish. The competitor, Marco, was a workhorse. He was fast, efficient, and careless.

The edges of display cases and walls where the scrubbing machine could not reach had to be scrapped with a heavy-duty razor blade. Marco's brother, who was working along with us, had a six-inch handle with a razor blade mounted on the end sticking out of his back pants pocket. He was bent over and Marco reached over him to get a mop and ran his arm from the wrist to the elbow across the razor blade. It was panic time as Marco was bleeding profusely and we were locked into the department store with no key to get out. Security precaution but a very bad idea. Long story short, we quickly got in touch with the store manager. Marco was rushed to the emergency room; it took 80 stiches to close the wound and he was back at work two hours later. That was either dedication or a whole lot of foolishness on his part, I believe it was the latter.

.

LEAF TALK

I love the fall of the year, not because the days get shorter and cooler but because of the beauty of everything. That time of year is one of the best things about living in the Northeast. Honking geese flying across a crystal blue sky heading for a warmer climate. Field speckled with orange pumpkins, all kinds of things apple - festivals, pies, butter, cider, jelly, and the list goes on and on. Wearing sweaters, light jackets, heavier wool socks, and corduroy pants in late autumn.

What excites me the most though is the beauty of the hardwood trees. They have center stage in this part of the world, especially during the months of September, October, and if you're fortunate, early November. Driving through the Berkshires, Poconos, Catskills, or any other Northeast mountain range, it looks as though someone from above poured cans of red, yellow, orange, and gold paint on the sides of the mountains. Driving can be hazardous as you can get so mesmerized by the gorgeous scenery. Better to park, breath the crisp mountain air, soak in the surroundings, and meditate.

If leaves could talk, and maybe they do in their own way, the maple leaf would speak the loudest. They are striking when they are green but spectacular as they make their way to a bland brown, fall off, and decompose. Probably the ones that fall off the earliest are the ones the others envy. We use to press fallen leaves between two sheets of wax paper and cover the glass on the outside doors and windows with them. Not only were they attractive, but also it made it impossible for others to look in and spy on you.

Raking leaves seemed an endless task though. Why can't they all drop at the same time? You rake your yard and it looks good until the next gust of wind blows in a new batch of leaves. There were no leaf blowers when I was young. Although raking could be tedious and tiresome, there was a peacefulness and serenity about it, so unlike the rumple and roar of a leaf blower. In the "old town" at that time, we could rake the leaves to the curb and burn them in the gutters. Even the smell of burning leaves added to the aura of autumn.

Alas though in December, the maple leaf must give way to the pine needle. The never changing pine needle becomes the center of attention during the holiday season. It does have a pleasant aroma, but what a waste to cut down a perfectly good tree, put it in your house for three or four weeks, and then send it to the curb for the garbage truck to pick up and take to the landfill. The maple tree loses its leaves, the pine loses its life.

THE SOFT CHOCOLATE ICE CREAM TRIPS

It had become a Sunday night ritual during the summer. About a dozen miles from the "old town" was a bigger old town that had an ice cream shop that was very popular. It was self-sustaining. A family farm with a large dairy herd produced enough product to not only provide dairy items for surrounding towns, but there was ample surplus left over to maintain a large ice cream shop.

Those summer Sunday evenings, my father would take the family, my grandmother included, on a drive through the mountains to the town with the famous ice cream shop. It was crowded in the car, a 1959 Rambler. In those days, wearing seat belts was optional. That being the case, there would be three people in the front seat, usually my mother, father, and sister. My brother and I sat in the back-bench seat with my grandmother. If my father was in a good mood and wanted to appease us kids, he would let us listen to the AM frequency radio as we drove through the countryside. The radio stations on AM at that time would usually play a round of about three minutes of commercials then three minutes of music. Of course, the volume would never be turned up too loud.

There was usually an argument, not a loud one though, on the way to the ice cream shop. It would be between my father and his mother over who was going to pay for the ice cream. She usually won out reasoning that her son had provided the transportation and the least she could do was pay for the ice cream. While the other family members would order sundaes or milk shakes, I always ordered a large soft chocolate ice cream cone. It was a masterpiece the way they would twist the ice cream, swirling it deep into the cone. I mentioned earlier the cleaning job where we enjoyed donuts, ice cream was also served there. The owner there had perfected swirling ice cream. He would start by swirling the ice cream on the outside edge of the cone. So although it appeared one got a lot of ice cream, it was an illusion. Not so with the shop we visited in my youth.

A big disappointment was the summer they stopped serving soft chocolate ice cream. I could not understand why. My father told me it was because they didn't sell enough of it. My reply was, "But I order it every time we come." An innocent, naïve child's remark. He just chuckled. The whole ritual would usually last about an hour and a half. A 30-minute drive to the ice cream shop, remember I mentioned my father was a very slow driver, 30 minutes to eat our ice cream, and a 30-minute ride back home. It was a pleasant experience that today would be considered nothing special and probably rather boring.

THE ICE CREAM SOCIAL

The volunteer fire department in the "old town" hosted ice cream socials three times during the summer. The socials were always held on a Sunday evening. On those Sunday evenings, we curtailed our trips to the famous ice cream shop. The purpose of the socials was not only to entertain and feed the town folks delicious ice cream, but they were very profitable fund raisers for the fire department. Gladys P. Childress and several other older ladies in the "old town" were in charge of making the ice cream. The first social was around Memorial Day, the second the middle of July, and the last close to Labor Day just before school was set to start. They would be held on the village green. The firemen would string up lights encircling the green and two rows coursing through the middle of the green. As a result, the green was well lit and quite picturesque. Along the outskirts would be the games of chance. The most popular was a booth where participants got two baseballs and the objective was to knock over six wooden milk bottles set up about 20 feet from the thrower. The milk bottles were stacked, three bottles as a base, two bottles placed on top of the base bottles, and one at the top forming a triangle. The objective was to knock over all six bottles with two throws. It was a challenge as the bottles were heavy and the baseballs were filled with sawdust rather than being the string woven type. The game was especially popular with us young boys as we tried to impress the girls with the speed and accuracy of our arm.

In the center of the green by the bandstand, tables and chairs were set up for playing bingo. There was a lot of gray hair playing bingo. The fire chief was the one who called out the letters and numbers to an enthusiastic crowd. As I mentioned earlier, he had emphysema. Just as he had difficulty barking out orders at a fire, his calls for the bingo games were also accompanied with a great deal of huffing and puffing. This led to confusion at times about what letters and numbers were actually called. When he was retired as fire chief, he was also retired as the caller at the bingo games.

The overpriced ice cream was the big drawing card. Served were the basic flavors, strawberry, chocolate, and vanilla in a cone or cup. There was no doubt that it was homemade as it was served right out of the canister. Strawberry was the most popular. The first social was right around harvest time for strawberries and whole strawberries, not crushed, were blended in the vanilla ice cream. It wasn't all about ice cream though. The firemen would grill hamburgers, hot dogs and sausage, peppers and onions accompanied with all kinds of condiments and beverages, non-alcoholic, of course. One can eat only so much ice cream. All would have a grand old time, and around 9:00 pm, things started to break up; the firemen began disassembling the concession stands and the town's residents headed back home. The last to leave were usually us young ones.

The socials fizzled out as the older generation died off. Who today would gather to eat ice cream, play bingo, and converse? In the social media age, an ice cream social does not stand a chance.

MY SOUTHERN EXPERIENCE

Between the years of 29 and 45, I lived in the South and this proved to be another enriching experience. Southerners like to give people nicknames, as a result there are a lot of Bubbas, Dukes, and Deweys. One day I was with a friend named Paul, and as we walked through his neighborhood, he said hello to Uncle Dump. He had known Uncle Dump all his life.

I asked him, "What's his real name?"

His reply, "I don't know, we have always just called him Uncle Dump." Nicknames catch on, you say, "MJ, Doctor J, Magic," and most people know exactly who you're talking about. You can tell I am an NBA junkie.

College basketball is huge in North Carolina, which is where I lived during my 16-year Southern hiatus. The best college basketball is played along tobacco road, which takes in the University of North Carolina, Duke, North Carolina State University, and Wake Forest. The two big ones though are the UNC Tar Heels and the Duke Blue Devils. The Tar Heels are probably the most popular team in the state, but Duke is the most popular nationally. Their rivalry continues to be the most intense in college basketball. To really appreciate this rivalry, you have to live there. It is one of those dates that you circled on your calendar when the two square off. Students literally camp outside Cameron Indoor Stadium for days to be able to attend a rivalry game, and the atmosphere makes it well worth the wait. The "Cameron Crazies" are among the most passionate fans in all of sports. They are very creative in their efforts to intimidate visiting opponents. During the time I lived there, the Charlotte Hornets came into existence. They were very popular but definitely took second place to the college teams. It is very rare for a professional team to take a back seat to a college team, but they did. Many probably do not remember who the first head coach was for the Hornets, but they know who Dean Smith, Mike Krzyzewski, and Jim Valvano were and are. I am not really sure which was more important in North Carolina religion or basketball.

Barbeque is right there with basketball, the two together make for an unbelievable experience. Pulled pork, course or sliced, brisket, and baby back ribs are foods I developed a love for and I mean love for. Just as important as the meat is the slaw and sauce. I prefer a vinegar-based slaw and a peppery sauce. I lived in a town that is famous for its style of barbeque. The population is approximately 30,000, but it has 25 to 30 barbeque stands and restaurants. Six days a week, never on Sunday, you smelled the aroma of barbeque as it is being smoked on open pits at the different restaurants.

Another delicacy was fried catfish, and as you got closer to the coast, oysters. I never developed much of a taste for either.

I don't get oysters, put some lemon juice or hot sauce on them and just swallow, no chewing. One time I watched a man sitting at a table next to me at a restaurant eat a tray of 25 oysters. I was amazed and grossed out at the same time.

The problem with catfish is that they are bottom feeders, and as a result, they eat some pretty nasty stuff. There was a man who lived just outside the town where I lived and he had a small pond behind his house. He would go fishing in a nearby larger lake usually at night and catch one catfish after another. He built cages somewhat similar to lobster traps, and when he got home, rather than cleaning the fish and freezing them, he would put them in cages in his little pond. Then he would feed them cornmeal figuring this would clean them out making for a healthier and tastier meal. Whenever he wanted catfish for dinner instead of going to the freezer, he went to the pond. Quite innovative.

Southern art, especially coastal paintings, really appeals to me. It puts you in a nice mood and you enjoy the scenery without the humidity. Some artist's works I enjoy are Mary O. Smith and Jeff Markowsky. Mary O. is gifted working with both water colors and oil. Both paint plein-air. An artist I long to have a work from is William Armstrong from Savanah, GA. I had an opportunity to visit his gallery and engage him in conversation. Very down to earth and interesting, but his paintings are way too expensive for me at present.

Things I did not like about the South are snakes, bugs, heat, and humidity. These will probably keep me from settling there again. An acquaintance who lived outside of town had a nice house with a large yard and garden space. When he mowed his grass, he would wear knee high heavy leather boots and have a pistol strapped to his side. The boots protected him from rattlesnake bites and the pistol was used to kill them. He told me one time when he was gathering corn from his garden he encountered a copperhead coiled around a cornstalk. Another friend was watching television one night and a little copperhead slithered out from under his sofa. The frightening thing is if you see a small copperhead, nearby is probably its mother. As for bugs, the one that I loathe is the tick. Once I was playing golf and went into the woods to fine an errant ball. The next day I noticed a tick attached to my leg, and shortly after that, followed a high fever and dizziness. I ended up taking medication for six weeks having to stay out of the sun. I became extremely cautious about going into the woods to retrieve a muffed shot from then on. That particular round of golf turned out to be very expensive. With regard to the heat and humidity for someone who grew up in the Northeast, it was oppressive during summer months. The first year I lived in North Carolina, we did not have air conditioning in our house. Sleeping or trying to sleep under a ceiling fan swirling around 90 degree + heat is to say the least very unpleasant. We did not repeat that experience the next year. I would rather do without a furnace in the winter than be without an air conditioner in the summer. When I lived in Arkansas, the temperatures were even hotter. When the weatherman reports that tomorrow will be a mild day in the low 90s, it's time to move.

 Something else that initially catches your attention in the South is river and lake water. It is brownish red in color from the clay and iron in the soil I suppose. The red soil would really make a mess of your car when you had to travel down a dirt road, especially after a rainfall. One time there were five of us out riding in a car with slick tires. The car slid into a ditch as we rounded a corner. We pushed the car out of the ditch, but the tires where flinging mud all over the place. When we got back to town, it was straight to the carwash. Not only did we wash off the car, but we hosed down each other as well. Actually it was quite refreshing as well as hysterical.

One of the greatest lessons I learned from my time in the South is the need for patience. Never rush a conversation. And never compare the way things are done up North with the way it's done down South. It is far better and more productive to first discuss the family, weather, or anything else but the main reason why you are trying to engage the person in conversation. I was in sales the last 14 years I lived in North Carolina, so it was a skill I had to master to survive. It was interesting to learn about people's struggles and the hard work they put in to build and maintain their business.

I recently visited with some friends from North Carolina. We had a grand time reminiscing. They are such good people and I look forward to the next opportunity to visit with them.

SOCKS, WHAT ARE SOCKS?

That question was raised by an Italian engineer named Anthony. Anthony was in North Carolina to install a kiln furnace in a tile plant where I did some work. We hit it off pretty well and I invited him over to our house for a meal. My wife is Italian and a fabulous cook. We had a good meal, good drink (Anthony brought an incredible wine), and good conversation. Anthony was interested in the area. We filled him in on the local cuisine (what to enjoy, what to stay away from), the culture of the people, and the textile industry. We mentioned a major product produced in the textile mills are socks. Thus came the question, "What are socks?" Socks in Italy would be pronounced calzini. I did not know that but Google did. After we figured it out, the conversation moved on to other subjects.

What are socks though? Used to be they were simply footwear, something to keep the feet warm, dry, and clean. Today, they are so much more. Men's hemlines have been raised to feature the sock. They are a fashion statement as well as an attention getter. I truly believe you can tell a lot about an individual's personality by the socks he wears. The same is probably true with women's hosiery.

Stripes are always popular, both vertical and horizontal. Some of the most outlandish socks I have ever seen was at a meeting of professional educators. One of the instructors reveled in wearing weird socks. The program lasted several days. Day one he was rather calm wearing a multi-colored vertical strip sock. Progressively, they became more bold and expressive, lighting bolts and rain drops were featured on day two. Day three though was over the top. He wore pink socks with little brown squirrels racing randomly around them. They definitely matched his personality as he was a very flamboyant and gregarious individual. I followed him on the program that day and felt compelled to pull up my pant leg and show off my plain black wool socks, which tells you something about my personality.

JOE – THE THREE LEGGED DOG

Joe was three-months-old when he came into my possession. He would punch at you with his front paws, thus he was named in honor of the boxer Joe Frazier. Joe was a redbone coon hound. Coon hounds have a remarkable bark and a propensity for roaming. I lived in a rural area when I got Joe and that was great for him. He was free to roam and bark wherever and whenever he wanted to.

Later, I move to town and rented an apartment. Three things that made it difficult living in town with Joe were his roaming habit was not appreciated and I felt bad having to cage him. Second, his bark irritated the neighbors, especially in the wee hours of the morning. And finally, he liked to stretch out on the hot asphalt in the middle of the road, which blocked traffic, fortunately I lived on a side street where cars had to go slow, otherwise Joe would have probably been a goner. For those reasons, I gave Joe to John, a good friend, who lived in the country and Joe was again happy and free to do as he pleased. All totaled Joe was my dog for about a year and a half.

John was great for Joe. John had an old pickup and would take Joe with him all the time. Joe was a riding fool. You would see him with his head hanging out of the open passenger's side window sniffing the air, sometimes letting out a howl. Occasionally, John and Joe came to town to visit with me. They would stay for an hour or two. John and I would have a beer and talk, Joe spent most of his time flopped on the couch, sleeping through most of the visit. He would jump up and race to the door when John would announce it was time to go. Joe had no desire to live back in town.

After John had Joe for a year or so, he had to move and could not take Joe with him. By this time, I was again living outside of town and Joe once again became my dog. He came though with only three legs. Joe liked to chase after anything that moved. John and I surmised that he was chasing a deer. Hunters do not take too kindly to that and we think one probably shot Joe resulting in his back-left leg having to be amputated. It was hard for John to tell me about Joe's misfortune. It was no fault of his, but he felt really bad and somewhat responsible. Being it was a back leg, Joe was still able to run and maneuver at a good speed. The funny thing was when he would chase after another dog, he would always nip at the dog's back legs.

Later, it became necessary for me to give Joe back to John, who was again in a position to take him and he readily welcomed having him back. Joe was a great dog and did not seem to mind going back and forth between John and me. He was loyal and easily adapted to both of us. If he had to choose, I think he would have picked John over me. Probably a big part of the reason why is because it was John who nursed Joe back to health after he had been shot. It was a very long and emotional recuperation. A second reason was that John took Joe for rides a lot more often than I did.

Every kid should have a Joe. And every Joe should have an owner like John.

JUNIOR BEAN AND

THE HAMBURGER HEIST

Let me first tell you about Junior Bean, then the town he watched over, and finally the hamburger heist. Junior rose to the rank of police chief in a sleepy North Carolina town. His predecessor was an ex-military officer who served as police chief for 20 years, long enough to qualify for a pension. Now able to double dip, having a pension from both the military and as a police officer, he could retire comfortably. He did not stay around town after retiring from the force. His retirement income allowed him to settle on the Outer Banks of North Carolina.

Junior worked under his predecessor for three years. The predecessor was well respected and he looked every bit the part of a police chief. He had kept himself in good physical shape. His uniform was always crisp and clean, shoes polished, shirt starched, and he often wore dark aviator sunglasses. A striking figure who people respected. Junior, on the other hand, looked anything but a police officer. He was short, 5'6" tall, and about

50 pounds overweight, tipping the scales somewhere around 215 lbs. What he lacked in physicality, he made up for with a burning desire to be a policeman. He knew the law, he knew it inside out. He showed the utmost respect to his superior always addressing him as "Chief." He had no problem working the most grueling schedule, the graveyard shift, where if there was going to be any serious trouble, it would be at that time of the night. There were only three deputies on the force and Junior proved to be by far the most zealous.

That being the case, when the predecessor retired, the mayor and three councilmen reluctantly went along with making Junior the new police chief. Whereas everyone called the predecessor "Chief," Junior was always just referred to as "Junior." I think this bothered him, but he did not let it show. His appearance did not inspire confidence. He wore a baggy uniform and clumsily played the role of police chief. He tried hard though, commendably he treated his deputies with great respect. He would often work the graveyard shift when he would not have had to do so. One night I was working a block up from the police station. It was early, around 8:00 pm. I saw Junior charge out of the station and slide across the hood of his police car that was in the reserved parking spot for the chief in front of the station. His best imitation of the Starsky and Hutch slide ended with him making it only half way across the hood, falling off and landing on his tailbone. Undeterred, he jumped up, got into his car, turned on the siren, and sped off. That was Junior.

The town he oversaw had three red lights and that was two more than what was really necessary. There were two banks, two restaurants, two supermarkets, and two gas stations. One of the restaurants was a pizza parlor run by a Laotian man, it was called Steve's Pizza. Interestingly, there were quite a few Laotians in the area. The owner of a shoe factory was not impressed by the work ethic of the locals and somehow he got in contact with a Laotian chieftain in Minnesota. He pursued the chieftain to bring along his villagers and move to North Carolina. The factory owner had 50 acres of land outside of town he let the Laotians settle on and set up a village. He also made it possible for them to purchase mobile homes from a local manufacturer at a very good price. The village was an interesting place. Several times I visited to just walk around and meet the people. Most of the older residents spoke limited English, but the younger ones would interpret for them. The Laotians did most of their cooking outside over a wood fire rather than using the stoves and ovens in their mobile homes. Bamboo was grown all over the village. The Laotians would cut stalks of bamboo about 18" long and cap off one end. The bamboo would be packed with rice and raisins and put in a fire pit. The moisture from the bamboo made the rice and raisins gooey and it easily slid out of the stalk. It was delicious and the Laotians were very hospitable in offering it to you. Each visit was always a pleasant experience. Besides the shoe factory, Junior's town also had a textile mill and a tile plant, which I mentioned in another story. Junior's town was a little bigger than my father's "old town."

The hamburger heist took place one summer night; it was a Wednesday night, sometime between 11:30 pm and 5:30 am. The scene of the crime was the other restaurant in town, the Burger Shed. I worked at the Shed Monday and Wednesday nights and on the weekend. My job was to mop the floor, empty trash, sweep the parking lot, and basically have the place ready for business the next day. It took me approximately two hours to perform my duties. I would show up about the time the last employee was ready to leave. He or she would empty the cash registers and wait for Junior or one of his deputies to escort them to one of the two banks to put the money in the night deposit box. After that I was on my own.

There were steel double doors at the back of the kitchen. I would go in and out of them to empty the mop water and put trash in the dumpster. The doors had hinges, which when I finished my work, I would place a thick, heavy duty metal bar about 5' long across the hinges on the inside of the double doors. This made it impossible for anyone to break into the restaurant through the kitchen. When my work was done, I would turn off the lights and exit through the front door, locking it behind me.

Thursday morning at 5:30 am when the morning crew came in to prep for opening, the bar was off the kitchen doors. Upon inspection, five cases of hamburgers were missing from the freezer along with a couple of boxes of chicken wings. Later that day, I was questioned by Junior and the owner about why the bar was not put on the kitchen doors. All I could say was that to the best of my recollection, I had secured the doors before I left. The general consensus though was that I had been negligent, and because I forgot to bar the doors, someone jimmied the lock, got in, and took the hamburger and chicken.

This was pretty big news in a little town and it got around town. I was allowed to keep working at the Shed but was still suspected of being careless about securing the restaurant the night of the hamburger heist. Junior made sure rounds were increased in town, checking doors and cruising pass other business establishments more often. Security was definitely heightened.

My vindication came three weeks later. Junior was on patrol and he spotted an empty hamburger case in the garbage beside the road outside a rundown house. Upon closer inspection, it was verified that it was from the Shed and the individual whose garbage it was in did not work at the Shed. Junior had his man. During the interrogation, Junior extracted from the thief how the crime went down. A young teenage boy named Brian had worked at the Shed. It was an after-school job. The owner of the Shed really liked Brian and put him in charge of the night crew. A husband and wife later were hired to work the evenings that Brian did not work. Over time it became obvious that the nights Brian did not work were much more profitable than the nights he did. As a result, Brian was eased out of his position, which he took offense to and quit. The problem was that Brian had the habit of giving his friends free food. When he quit, he purposely forgot to turn in his key, saying he loss it. He gave the key to the thief who went in the front door, locked it behind him, took the food from the freezer out the kitchen door, leaving the bar off to the side to make it look like I had forgot to secure the restaurant. Junior had me come by the station and he proudly explained everything. I told him I was very grateful and impressed with his detective work.

Junior did not remain police chief for very long. As I mentioned, he was overweight as well as a rather nervous type of individual. The stress of trying to measure up to his predecessor was probably a contributing factor in his having a serious heart attack. After that he never came back to work and the town council quickly moved on promoting one of his deputies as its new police chief. Solving the hamburger heist was the crowning accomplishment of Junior's tenure as police chief. It is a good thing we didn't have someone like Junior as constable in the "old town" when I was growing up.

DETROIT

I love Detroit, had the privilege of living there for three years. In a way, it resembles a Southern city. Many workers migrated from the South to Detroit, coming to work in the car factories back in the day. As a result, there are some very good soul food restaurants and a lot of Baptist churches in Detroit. The music is over the top good and the artist for the most part are real. I got to know a prolific writer and producer for Motown. Played golf with him occasionally and he introduced me to some who are considered Motown giants. It's so cool that you had young boys and girls mostly in their teens who turned their love for singing into a sheer delight for millions, the Motown sound. They worked hard traveling, performing, promoting their company and sound, they even stuffed their vinyl records into paper sleeves. If you get to Detroit, it's worth touring Hitsville, USA, the house where it all began.

Detroit has passionate sports fans, somewhat similar to Boston but much gentler. I remember it being said that "Detroit is a good beer drinking town in search of a professional football team." They have the Lions and their diehard fans have to be some of the most loyal ever, the Lions haven't won a championship since 1957. I would love to be there when or if they ever do.

Something else notable about Detroiters is they know how to dress. On average they spend about 50% more on fashion each year than the average American. Henry the Hatters is the place to go if you need of something to cover your head. You can spend hours there trying on one hat after another and they don't mind you taking your time to decide. The staff is very expertise and most generous with their time and attention.

Once some friends invited me to go clothes shopping with them. We were shopping for suits and they wanted me to buy a gold one. I'm not a gold suit guy, but one of them was. He purchased a gold suit; to go along with the suit, he bought gold shoes and a gold tie. Quite a striking sight, you might say he was golden. Really though, it is refreshing to see ones express themselves in neat, colorful fashion.

A very interesting section of Detroit is Hamtramck. It is the essence of cool. At one time, it was an enclave for people of Polish decent. There are still some excellent Polish restaurants in Hamtramck, my favorite is Under the Eagle at 9000 Joseph Campau Street. It was there that I was introduced to dill pickle soup. There are some great bakeries there as well. People from miles around come to Hamtramck bakeries on Fat Tuesday to buy and devour paczkis. In fact, in Hamtramck, it is referred to as Paczki Day. They were not my favorite, but one thing I did enjoy that was sold there is chocolate candies with vodka inside them. You can't eat many of those and be under the legal limit to drive.

When I lived in Detroit, Hamtramck was the first stop for most refugees or immigrants coming to Detroit. The second and third generation of Polish descendants had moved to the suburbs. Hamtramck was somewhat like the United Nations. In a two square mile area, there were 38 different languages spoken. Most seemed to respect one another, although ethnic difficulties aboard sometimes were expressed there.

Hamtramck Disneyland is worth a visit. It is a folk art installation created by Dmytro Szylak in the backyard of his home. He died in 2015 and now Hatch Art owns the property and maintains the installation.

Another Detroit staple is Buddy's Pizza. Their specialty is the Detroit-style pizza. It's probably the first known square pizza in the United States. It has crunchy, cheesy corner slices and a unique layering structure. There are about 15 locations now but go to the one at 17125 Conant Street in Detroit.

I love Detroit for the food, fashion, music, sports, vibe, and especially the people. To get the vibe, I suggest you listen to Mayer Hawthorne's song, "A Long Time." It's on his album, "How Do You Do."

SAGE SAYINGS

The following are two of the wisest statements I have ever heard. The first was uttered by a friend with a Jewish background. We will call him Saul. Saul was in his late 60s at the time, so he had garnered quite a bit of life experience. His advice was: "If you don't have to get credit for everything you do, you can get a lot done." Saul had gotten a lot done in his lifetime. He was well educated, started several successful businesses, and had a real knack for figuring out people.

This experience shows how savvy Saul is. One of Saul's businesses was a tool and dye shop. He is a very patient man who speaks with a gentle mildness, even in tense situations. One young employee felt he could manipulate Saul because of his meek personality. Tardiness and minor employee thief were overlooked by Saul on a couple of occasions. When the young employee verbally assaulted Saul's secretary something had to be done.

Saul invited the employee into his office, had him sit down, and calmly told him, "Son, you made a very big mistake. You mistook kindness as being a sign of weakness. You have 15 minutes to pack up your belongings and get out of here and never come back." The young man apologized profusely and pleaded with Saul not to fire him. All Saul said was, "You're down to 12 minutes." Saul was not a man to be messed with.

I would imagine you have come across individuals who will go out of their way to let others know about their supposed accomplishments. I have, and after a while, I just roll my eyes and think, you fool. A wise proverb says, "Let someone else praise you, and not your own mouth; Others and not your own lips." Pretty good counsel, I'm sure Saul would agree.

The other statement came from a Hispanic gentleman named Enrique. Enrique had enjoyed quite a few well-deserved privileges and responsibilities. He was at a point in life where he had to relinquish some of these because of age and other circumstances. At the time, I had just received a tremendous advancement that came with outstanding perks, ones similar to what Enrique was now giving up. I asked him what advice he had for me.

His reply was, "When you're going up, make sure you're nice to the ones coming down." His point was that someday I would be the one coming down.

I never forgot that and have tried hard to show dignity and respect especially to my elders. I am now at the point where I have started a slow decent downward. It can be hard to let go of cherished privileges and responsibilities and I know that soon I will have to let go of even more. Although I will miss these, I am happy for the ones who will get the opportunity to do the things that I loved doing. I hope I can keep that attitude and not lament the things I am no longer able to do but just enjoy and do my best at the things I can do.

MY BROTHER'S CALLS

After our mother died, my brother and I went back to our far different routines with little contact. Occasionally, I receive a text from him regarding something he heard about the "old town" or about one of our relatives. If it's a phone call, I know someone has probably died. His last call was to inform me that Mike is now resting in peace. Mike, Nick and I were super tight growing up and now I am the only one left. After each of us left the "old town," we hardly ever saw one another again. What I have is distant memories of three crazy young kids, one of which would do a lot of things differently if he had it to do all over again.

Mike was the oldest of us three by a year, he was a grade ahead of Nick and me. Mike moved like a sloth, no doubt the heavy use of tobacco and other substances contributed to that, but so did his upbringing. His parents worked him like a hired laborer. He had a younger brother and older sister who were pampered compared to Mike. When he should have been playing with the other kids in the "old town," instead he was working from sun up to sun down on his grandfather's farm just outside of the "old town." At times Nick and I would go to the farm to help Mike with his chores, so he could get done early and join us for some revelry. I truly believe that by age 18 Mike was physically burned out. My brother saw Mike about three years before he died and said he looked pretty rough. His father had died and Mike, his brother, and sister came to the "old town" to bury him. That was his last trip there as he had taken up residence in Florida.

Mike had a criminal record. All three of us had done some very dishonest things, Mike was the only one who got caught. He had started breaking into a farm machinery shop in the "old town" and skimming a little off the top of the cash register. It was an easy place to break into, but about the fourth or fifth time he did a real police officer (a State Police detective) turned on the lights and arrested him. He stuck a gun in Mike's face and ask him who else ever broke into the shop. Panic caused Mike to give up the name of another "old town" youth named Harry. Harry was promptly arrested the next day. Harry had been breaking into the farm machinery shop long before Mike. In fact he introduced Mike to the free money. Harry accused Mike of ratting him out, but Harry would have done the same thing if the tables were turned. And it would not have taken a gun in the face for Harry to voluntarily give up names and information if he thought it would lessen his punishment. I didn't care much for Harry, he was big in stature, a bully, and a liar. To show the degree of his lying, he bragged one Monday morning in school how on Saturday night he drank two six-packs of beer and a quart of Wild Cherry Mist. That was insane, three grown men probably could not drink that much alcohol in one night. He was the only one who believed his lies. It didn't hurt my feelings to see Harry get busted, but I felt for Mike. The couple who owned the farm machinery shop knew Mike, his grandfather had done business with them for decades and they were devastated. This incident contributed to Mike's leaving the "old town" as soon as he could and rarely returning.

THE AUTHOR

Peter Perrin is my pen name. Most of the characters' names mentioned in "How I Got, Where I Am" have been changed as well. You have to protect the innocent.

I seek neither fame nor fortune, although some pesos from the sale of this book would be nice. A wise man said, "Give me neither poverty nor riches." The poverty part is easy to understand but few have seen the reason not to strive for riches. From my viewpoint, I see that with riches could come slavery to them. In a way that is Biblical and definitely true. I have seen ones enjoy their material assets, nothing wrong with that, but afraid to leave their comfort zone. I think that is especially true of generational wealth and businesses. The patriarch starts a business, works hard, it becomes successful, and it's assumed the children will follow in his footsteps and the grandchildren after them, etc.

This can lead to some nice material rewards, but it can also become a spider's web, one almost impossible to escape from. Nice material rewards probably kept some in or around the "old town," too comfortable to venture from a good situation.

I feel one of life's greatest treasures is experiencing different cultures and customs and not just on a vacation but actually living it. I have acquired wonderful friends from every corner of the earth. As a result, I have learned about scotch bonnet, shawarma, hushallsost, and other delicacies. I marvel at the positive attitude and appreciation of ones who spent years in refugee camps and did not allow the experience to embitter them. I have had some unbelievable acts of kindnesses shown to me by ones who are far less fortunate than me and they considered it a privilege to do so. In imitation of them, I have also experienced the joy of giving of oneself in behalf of others. A real blessing for a wayward boy from the "old town."

If you have read this book, thank you. It has been said that everyone has one good book in them. This may not be a good book, but it might be my one and only book. I doubt others will follow as time seems too precious to spend writing about myself, my experiences, and viewpoints. But please pass along your life stories, so that others can benefit from the wisdom and experiences you have gained. Also, take the time to make memories so that in the so-called golden years you have something to reflect back on rather than lament about. What a shame it would be if toward the end of one's life, he or she had to say, "I wish I had done this or that." So, make your own memories, don't revel in the memories of others.

Reflect on the good things in life, the bad things will take care of themselves. Time can suppress them, if not totally erase them from memory. Also in my opinion, it is better to drink white wine rather than red wine or beer. Wine has far few calories than beer. In older age, you have to make your calories count. As to why white wine is better than red, spill both on a carpet and you will see why. Another thing I have come to appreciate is a good cup of coffee. In lieu of driving a luxury car or wearing Armani suits, splurging on a quality cup of coffee is a small price to pay. One must be reasonable if one is to live a long time. And that is a good way to be known as a reasonable person.

In conclusion, I like where I am at right now. Not a perfect place but an enjoyable one. It's not so much a place as it is a situation. How I got where I am is in large part due to the experiences and people I grew up with in the "old town." I sense them now only in the recesses of my mind being physically and emotionally far removed from the "old town." I try not to live in the past but learn from it, and hopefully become wiser and a more patient person. That also would be a nice way to be known.